RUBANK EDUCATIONAL LIBRARY No. 160

T0081621

SELECTED STUDIES

Advanced Etudes, Scales and Arpeggios in All Major and Minor Keys

by H. Voxman

ADVANCED ETUDES

	Page		Page
C Major	2	A Minor	4
F Major	6	D Minor	8
G Major	10	E Minor	12
B♭ Major	14	G Minor	16
D Major	18	B Minor	20
E♭ Major	22	C Minor	24
A Major	26	F♯ Minor	28
A♭ Major	30	F Minor	32
E Major	34	C♯ Minor	36
D♭ Major	38	B♭ Minor	40
B Major	42	G♯ Minor	44
F♯ Major	46	D♯ Minor	48
C♯ Major	50	A♯ Minor	52

SCALES AND ARPEGGIOS

Scales 55
Chromatic Study 61
Arpeggios 62

SPECIAL STUDIES

Velocity 54
Interval Studies 65
Tonguing Studies 68
Cadenza Studies 72

RUBANK®

HAL•LEONARD® CORPORATION

7777 W. Bluemound Rd. P.O. Box 13819 Milwaukee, WI 53213

C Major

GALLAY

Copyright MCMLII by Rubank, Inc., Chicago, IL
International Copyright Secured

BÖHME

A Minor

BLAZHEVICH

Moderato
f pesante
p
f
p
f

F Major

DUHEM

Marcia
mf
dolce
f
f
f
mf
mf
f
mf

D Minor

BÖHME

Andante

f

simile

p

tr

BLAZHEVICH

Moderato

f *deciso*

p

cresc.

To Coda

f

ff
f
cresc.
ff
D.C. al Coda
rit.
Coda
poco agitato e string.
p
cresc.
f
p
ff
poco rit.

G Major

Larghetto cantabile
p
rall.
p a tempo
f
a tempo
rall.
p a tempo
rall.
f
a tempo
rall.
p
tr
p
rall.

MÜLLER

Allegro moderato

E Minor

BÖHME

Allegro moderato
pp
più sensibile
[more expressively]
cresc. a poco a poco
f
p espressivo e con passione
agitato e cresc.
f
smorz.
tratt.
[held back]
p agitato
ff
p
ff
p
f
ff
f
p
smorz.
pp

B♭ Major

GATTI

BÖHME

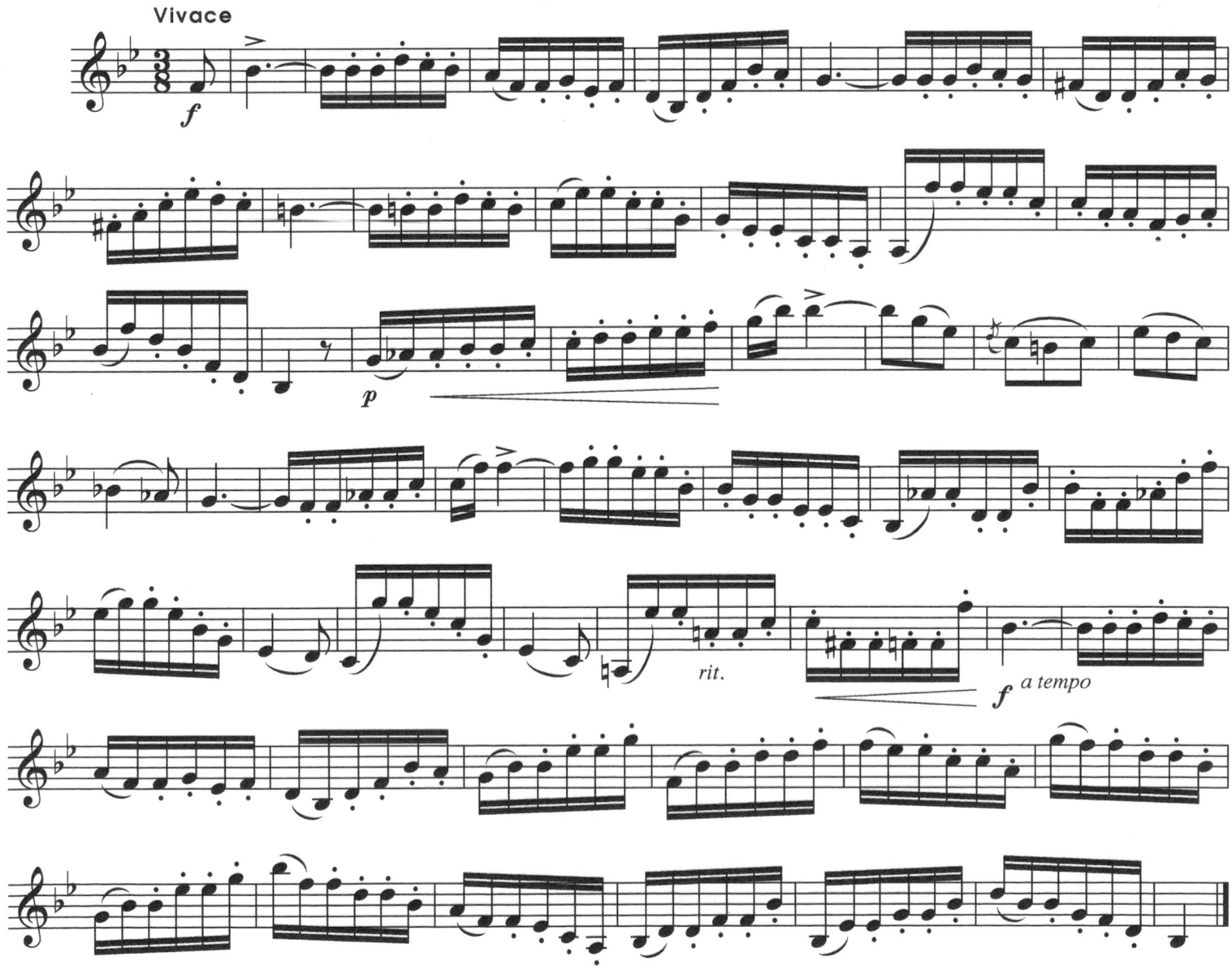

G Minor

BOHME

BLAZHEVICH

D Major

GATTI
Largo cantabile
pp
f lebile
afrett. [accel.]
rinf.
tratt.
f
ten.
pp a tempo
cresc.
f
pp
stent.
f
p a tempo
smorz.
pp
morendo
ROSSARI
Allegro giusto
f
p

poco rall.
a tempo
f

B Minor

ROSSARI

GATTI

Allegretto grazioso
p
f
p
f
p
cresc. poco a poco
pp
cresc. poco a poco
f
f
sempre stacc.
f
p
ff
sempre stacc.
ff
smorz.
dim.

E♭ Major

BLAZHEVICH

C Minor

CAPRICCIO

St. JACOME

Allegretto
p legére
mf
pp
p
p
mf

A Major

Andante con moto
BLAZHEVICH
p dolce
p
p
p
dolce
f
rit.
Tempo I
p
p
p
f
p
f
p
cresc.
rit.

MÜLLER

F♯ Minor

BÖHME

Maestoso
ff energicamente
pp
ff
pp
f
p
f
p
pp
ff
pp
ff
pp
ff
pp
cresc. poco a poco
f
ff
pp
p scherzando con grazia
sf
p
sf
p
cresc. poco a poco
rinf.
ff
pp
ppp
cresc.
ff

A♭ Major

DUHEM

BÖHME

F Minor

BLAZHEVICH

Allegro mosso
ff vigoroso
f
p
cresc.
f
p
f
p
cresc. poco a poco
f
p
cresc. poco a
poco
f
p
pp
cresc.
f

E Major

FEDOROW

Giocoso
BLAZHEVICH
f
p
f
p
f
Fine
Poco meno mosso
p sostenuto
f
p
poco a poco accel.
D. S. al Fine
f

C♯ Minor

ROSSARI

Allegro
mf
p
p
rit.
Tempo I
mf
p
f
p
p

D♭ Major

BÖHME

ROSSARI

B♭ Minor

BÖHME

SCHERZO

BAGANTZ

B Major

BIMBONI

Tempo di polacca
FEDOROW
f
mf
f
ff
mf
f
Fine
TRIO
p
cresc.
f
p
f
D.C. al Fine

G♯ Minor

Andante con spirito
BAGANTZ
p
sf
p
sf
f risoluto
p
f
p
p
p
p
f
p
poco a poco dim.
morendo e rallentando

Poco agitato (Allegro)
p
p
p
p
1.
2.
p
p

F♯ Major

DIEPPO
Allegretto
p
dolce
a tempo
mf
rall.
p a tempo
scherzando
cresc.
f
tr

BLAZHEVICH

D♯ Minor

BLAZHEVICH

BLAZHEVICH

C♯ Major

ROSSARI

JOHANSON

A♯ Minor

ROSSARI

Allegro (𝅗𝅥 = 1 beat)
f
p
mf
f
Tempo I
p
p
f
dim.
p
f
f
ff
rit.

Velocity

St. JACOME
(adapted)

Scales

The use of a metronome with the following studies is highly recommended.

C MAJOR

A MINOR (melodic form)*

F MAJOR

D MINOR

* All minor scale exercises should also be practiced in the harmonic form.

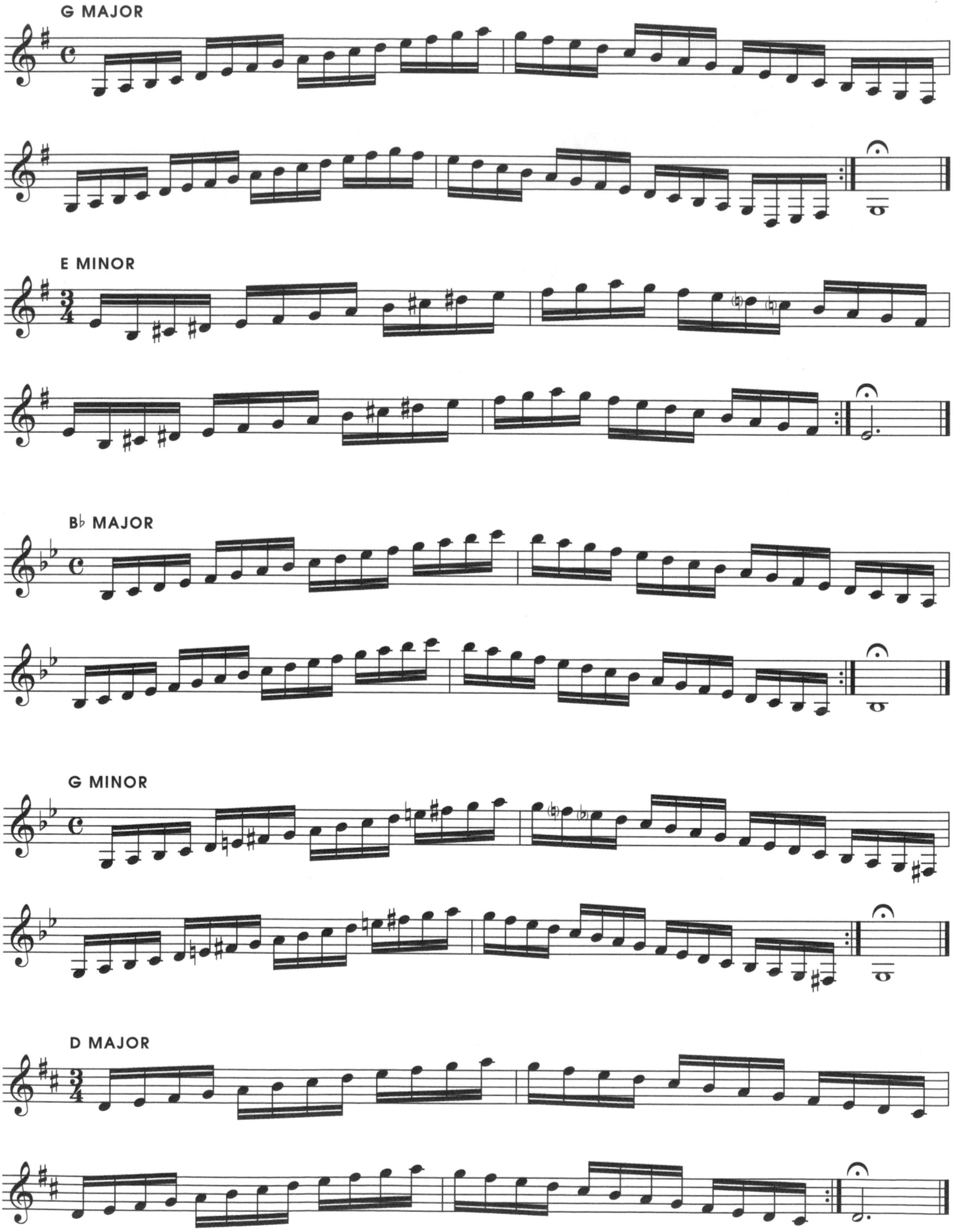
G MAJOR
E MINOR
B♭ MAJOR
G MINOR
D MAJOR

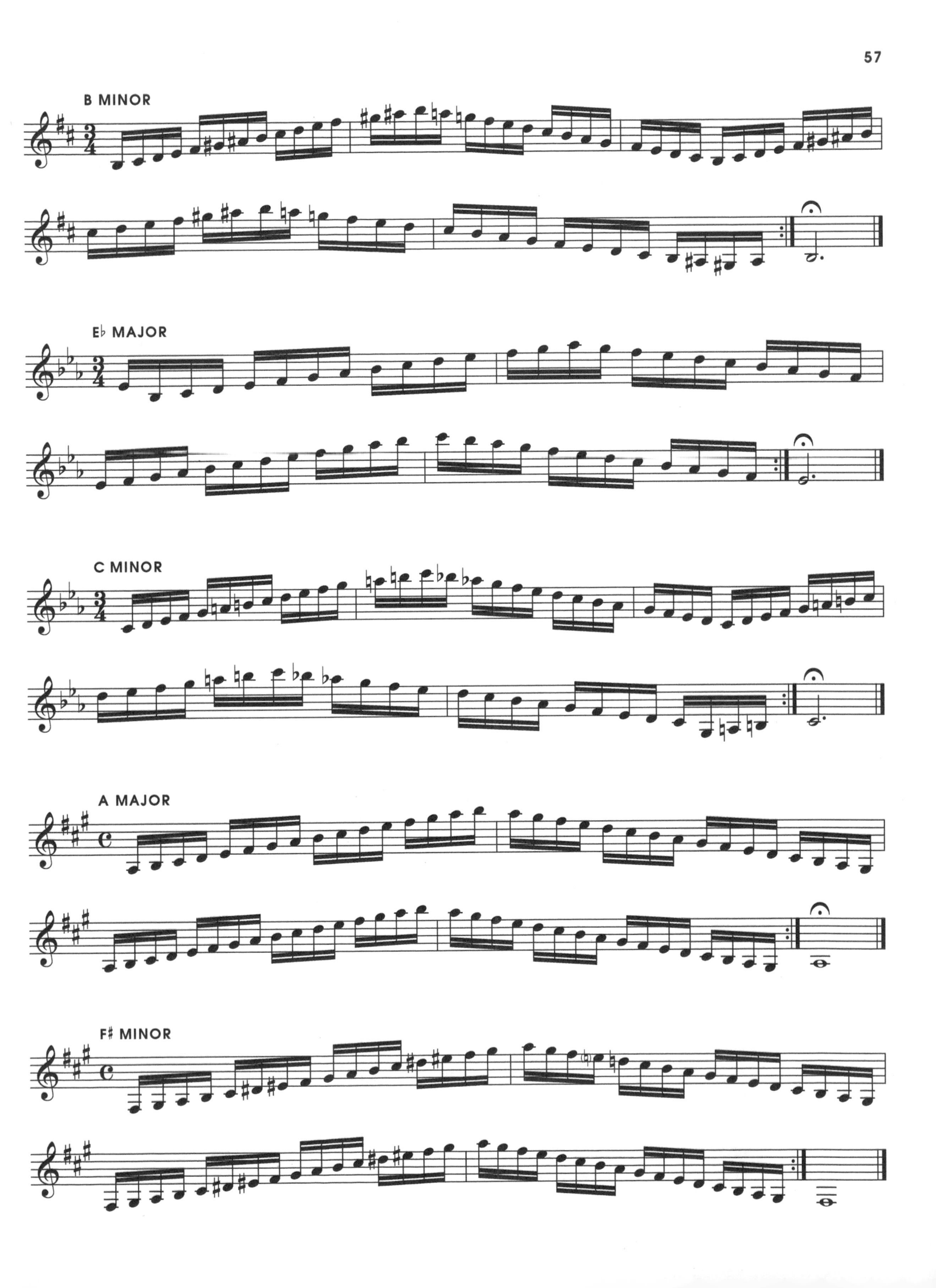
B MINOR
E♭ MAJOR
C MINOR
A MAJOR
F♯ MINOR

A♭ MAJOR
F MINOR
E MAJOR
C♯ MINOR
D♭ MAJOR

B♭ MINOR
B MAJOR
G♯ MINOR
F♯ MAJOR
D♯ MINOR

C♯ MAJOR

A♯ MINOR

Whole tone scale on F♯

Whole tone scale on G

Chromatic Scales

Chromatic Study

BÖHME

Arpeggios

(a)
(b)
(c)
(d)
C MAJOR
A MINOR
F MAJOR
D MINOR
G MAJOR
E MINOR
B♭ MAJOR
G MINOR

D MAJOR
B MINOR
E♭ MAJOR
C MINOR
A MAJOR
F♯ MINOR
A♭ MAJOR
F MINOR
E MAJOR
C♯ MINOR

C♯ MAJOR
A♯ MINOR
B MAJOR
G♯ MINOR
F♯ MAJOR
D♯ MINOR
C♯ MAJOR
A♯ MINOR
Arpeggio of the augmented 5th

Interval Studies

BAGANTZ

ARBAN

Apply to exercises 3 – 10:
ARBAN
(a)
(b)
(c)
3
4
5
6
7
8
9
10
Allegro
simile
CORNETTE
11

Tonguing Studies

CHAVANNE

ad lib.
a tempo
p
leggiero

Allegro moderato
Single and triple tonguing
CHAVANNE
p
f
mf
tr
p
mf

p
mf
mf
mf
p
f
brillante
f
f

Cadenza Studies